NEW SMALL APARTMENTS

NOUVEAUX PETITS APPARTEMENTS

NEUE KLEINE APARTMENTS

NEW SMALL APARTMENTS
NOUVEAUX PETITS APPARTEMENTS
NEUE KLEINE APARTMENTS

evergreen

© 2008 EVERGREEN GmbH, Köln

Editorial coordination:
Simone Schleifer

Editorial assistant:
Mariana R. Eguaras Etchetto

Texts:
Florian Seidel

Translations coordinator:
Carla Parra Escartín for Cillero & de Motta, Saragossa

English translation:
Juan Antonio Ripoll, Elizabeth Jackson for Cillero & de Motta, Saragossa

French translation:
Anthony Rousseau, Céline Brandy for Cillero & de Motta, Saragossa

German proof-reading:
Cillero & de Motta, Saragossa

Text editing:
José Jóvena Casañ for Cillero & de Motta, Saragossa

Art director:
Mireia Casanovas Soley

Graphic design and layout:
Ignasi Gracia Blanco

Printed in Spain

ISBN 978-3-8365-0830-8

Contents Sommaire Inhalt

It is a great challenge for any designer to take a small apartment and create within it the sensation of space characteristic of a large upper-class apartment or even a house. It is precisely when there is little available space that architects must draw on all of their inventiveness and creative ability. Imagination and creativity are needed to give a reduced area unexpected size and make limited space seem larger, lighter and more varied than it actually is. In the end, all dwellings must offer the same things – a place to sleep, eat, relax and satisfy the need for personal cleanliness. However, no two dwellings are the same; they are all made different by the individual ideas, desires and dreams of the people residing in them.

At the turn of the twentieth century, how to solve the problem of the housing shortage affecting the population of Europe became a fundamental question. In most cases, the only practical solution seemed to be optimization of small apartments, which had architects constantly seeking inspiration in new areas. The famous *Frankfurt kitchen*, the first fitted kitchen in the world, began as an adaptation of the kitchen found in train dining cars and applied to the construction of housing. Architects were likewise inspired by Japanese models and experimented with living rooms that turned into bedrooms at night with the help of versatile built-in closets and curtains.

At the same time, but on a completely different although no less interesting path, the Austrian architect Josef Frank took a critical stance against the rationalist efforts of his contemporaries. Still convincing today is his unconventional argument that a non-optimized dwelling seems larger than one where space is made perfect use of. If one is made to pass through the dwelling again and again when carrying out daily tasks, even in a round-about way, then that person inevitably has the feeling that there is more room. Only a dwelling that is experienced through daily use, i.e. a non-optimized one, leaves a memory of place.

In response to the need to obtain maximum quality of life from the smallest spaces, various options are also available today. Intelligent use of lighting, proportion and color create spaces that make you forget the limitations of size. Elsewhere, the structure of the dwelling is modified by a spatial motif, an unusual material, a bright color, a sculptural shape or a unique detail. In this book, we show how large residential oases can be created in a small space by placing intentional emphasis on flexibility, through the different possible ways of making good use of a single space, and also by means of movable features.

Donner à un petit logement une sensation d'espace digne d'un grand appartement bourgeois ou même d'une maison n'est pas tâche facile pour un concepteur. C'est précisément lorsque l'espace disponible est réduit que l'architecte doit faire appel à toute son imagination et sa capacité créatrice. Il faut donc de la fantaisie et de la créativité pour offrir une amplitude inattendue à un local réduit et faire qu'un espace limité paraisse plus grand, plus lumineux et plus varié que ce qu'il est en réalité. En fin de compte, tous les logements doivent offrir la même chose : un endroit où dormir, manger, se détendre et se laver. Cependant, aucune habitation ne ressemble à une autre, chacune d'entre elles se différencie par les idées, les désirs et les rêves concrets de ses occupants.

Au début du XXe siècle, mettre un terme au problème du manque de logements dont souffrait la population devint une question fondamentale en Europe. Dans la plupart des cas, la seule solution satisfaisante était d'optimiser l'espace des petits logements, d'où une recherche permanente de la part des architectes de nouvelles sources d'inspiration : la fameuse « cuisine de Francfort », la première cuisine modulaire au monde, constituait à l'origine l'adaptation à la construction de logements des cuisines de wagons-restaurants. Au même moment, certains architectes, s'inspirant de modèles venus du Japon, expérimentèrent des salons qui se transformaient en chambres à coucher la nuit, grâce à des rideaux ou des armoires encastrées flexibles.

L'architecte autrichien Josef Frank adopta à cette époque une démarche complètement différente, mais tout aussi intéressante, en gardant une attitude très critique à l'égard des efforts rationalistes de ses contemporains. Son argument peu conventionnel reste convaincant même de nos jours : une habitation dont l'espace n'est pas optimisé semble plus grande que celle qui occupe parfaitement l'espace. Si nous sommes obligés, lors des tâches quotidiennes, de parcourir l'ensemble du logement à plusieurs reprises, et parfois même en faisant des détours, nous avons automatiquement la sensation que l'espace est plus grand. Seul reste gravé dans notre mémoire l'appartement dans lequel on vit consciemment pour l'usage quotidien, c'est-à-dire l'habitation qui n'est pas optimisée.

Ainsi aujourd'hui, diverses possibilités sont également proposées pour répondre au besoin d'obtenir une qualité de logement maximale à partir d'un espace réduit. L'utilisation intelligente de la lumière, de la proportion et de la couleur permet de créer des lieux de vie qui font oublier les limites imposées par l'espace. D'autre part, une certaine approche de l'espace, un matériau peu habituel, une couleur voyante, une forme structurelle ou encore un détail singulier modifient la structure du logement. Cet ouvrage démontre qu'en accentuant intentionnellement la flexibilité il est possible de créer de vates paradis dans un espace réduit, grâce à la possibilité d'aménager un espace unique de différentes manières, mais également grâce à l'utilisation d'éléments mobiles.

Einem kleinen Apartment etwas von der Großzügigkeit einer großen, bürgerlichen Wohnung oder sogar eines eigenen Hauses zu verleihen, ist eine besondere Herausforderung für jeden Designer. Gerade wenn der zur Verfügung stehende Raum knapp ist, sind Erfindungsreichtum und das gestalterische Vermögen des Architekten gefordert. In der Enge eine unerwartete Weite erfahrbar zu machen, den beschränkten Raum größer, lichter, abwechslungsreicher wirken zu lassen, als er wirklich ist, erfordert Fantasie und Kreativität. Jede Wohnung muss letztlich das gleiche bieten: einen Platz zum Schlafen, zum Essen, zum Entspannen und für die Körperpflege; dennoch ist keine Wohnung wie die andere, denn zu unterschiedlich sind die individuellen Vorstellungen, Wünsche und Träume der jeweiligen Bewohner.

Zu Beginn des 20. Jahrhunderts rückte in Europa die Frage in den Mittelpunkt, wie man die Wohnungsnot der Bevölkerung beenden könnte. Meist schien die Optimierung der Kleinstwohnung die einzig sinnvolle Lösung zu sein, für die die Architekten Inspiration auf immer neuen Gebieten suchten: Die berühmte „Frankfurter Küche", die erste Einbauküche der Welt, war im Prinzip die Übertragung der Speisewagenküche in den Wohnungsbau. Zugleich experimentierten Architekten, inspiriert von Vorbildern aus Japan, mit Wohnräumen, die sich für die Nachtruhe mithilfe flexibler Wandschränke oder Vorhänge in Schlafräume verwandeln ließen.

Einen völlig anderen, jedoch nicht minder interessanten Weg beschritt zur gleichen Zeit der österreichische Architekt Josef Frank, der den Rationalisierungsbestrebungen seiner Zeitgenossen sehr kritisch gegenüber stand. Seine ungewöhnliche Argumentation ist auch heute noch überzeugend: Eben die nicht-optimierte Wohnung wirkt größer als eine Wohnung, die den Raum perfekt ausnutzt. Ist man gezwungen, bei seinen täglichen Verrichtungen immer wieder durch die ganze Wohnung zu gehen, vielleicht sogar auf Umwegen, wird zwangsläufig die Wohnung als größerer Raum erfahren. Nur die Wohnung, die im täglichen Gebrauch bewusst erlebt wird, also nicht optimiert ist, prägt sich als Ort ein.

So bieten sich zur Lösung der Frage, wie man auf kleinstem Raum ein Maximum an Wohnwert schafft, auch heute unterschiedliche Wege an. Durch den geschickten Einsatz von Licht, Proportion und Farbe werden Orte geschaffen, die die räumlichen Einschränkungen vergessen lassen. Andernorts gliedert ein bestimmtes räumliches Motiv, ein außergewöhnliches Material, eine auffallende Farbe, eine skulpturale Form oder ein besonderes Detail die Wohnung. In diesem Band wird gezeigt, wie es durch die bewusste Betonung von Flexibilität, durch die Möglichkeit, ein und denselben Raum auf vielfache Weise zu nutzen, aber auch durch den Einsatz beweglicher Elemente möglich wird, auf kleinstem Raum große Wohnoasen zu schaffen.

NEW SMALL APARTMENTS
NOUVEAUX PETITS APPARTEMENTS
NEUE KLEINE APARTMENTS

Residence Chen

CJ Studio

The concept of this apartment is based on the idea of a single space with clearly-defined, separate areas. The changes in ceiling height, split level flooring and an S-shaped partition wall have smooth and elegant lines that subtly accentuate the different zones of the dwelling. The curved wall is the most important element of the apartment. It separates the entrance, living room and kitchen, i.e. the common areas, from the private areas consisting of the bedroom, bathroom and office. Both sides of the partition can be used as a built-in closet. White and different pastel shades are the defining colors in this apartment. The sheen of the walls, ceilings and floors make the apartment look larger than it really is.

Le concept de cet appartement se base sur l'idée d'un espace unique qui présente cependant des zones définies nettement séparées. Les variations de hauteur de plafond, les différences de niveau du sol et une cloison en forme de S affichent des lignes légères et élégantes qui font ressortir de manière subtile les différentes zones du logement. La cloison courbe constitue l'élément le plus important de cet appartement. Elle sépare l'entrée, le salon et la cuisine, c'est-à-dire les pièces communes du logement, des parties privées : la chambre, la salle de bains et un bureau. Chaque côté de la cloison peut recevoir un placard encastré. Les couleurs dominantes de ce logement varient entre le blanc et diverses tonalités claires. L'éclatante luminosité des murs, des plafonds et des sols créent l'impression d'un appartement plus grand qu'il ne l'est réellement.

Das Konzept dieses Apartments basiert auf der Idee eines einzigen Raumes, der dennoch bestimmte, klar getrennte Bereiche aufweist. Höhenvorsprünge in der Decke, Niveauunterschiede im Fußboden und eine S-förmige Trennwand weisen eine weiche, elegante Linienführung auf und betonen auf subtile Weise die verschiedenen Zonen der Wohnung. Die gebogene Trennwand ist das wichtigste Element des Apartments. Sie trennt Eingangsbereich, Wohnzimmer und Küche, also die öffentlichen Zonen der Wohnung, von den privaten Bereichen, die Schlafzimmer, Bad und einen Arbeitsraum umfassen. Von beiden Seiten kann die Trennwand als Einbauschrank genutzt werden. Weiß und diverse helle Farbtöne sind die bestimmenden Farben der Wohnung: Die alles überstrahlende Helligkeit der Wände, Decken und Fußböden lässt das Apartment größer wirken als es tatsächlich ist.

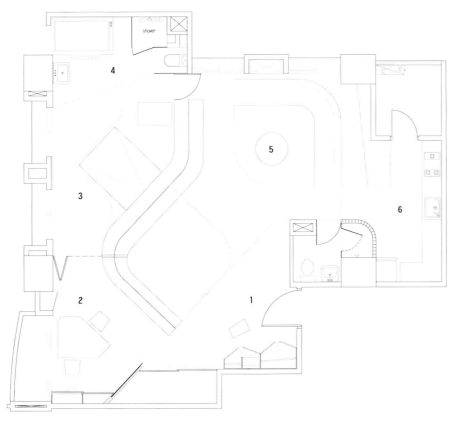

shower

4

3

2

5

6

1

Plan Plan Grundriss

The diagonally laid out work space and the bath open to the bedroom were specially designed for the owners.

Le bureau, placé en diagonale, et la salle de bains ouverte sur la chambre ont été réalisés sur demande expresse du propriétaire.

Der diagonal gestellte Arbeitsplatz und das zum Schlafzimmer offene Bad sind auf besonderen Wunsch der Bauherren entstanden.

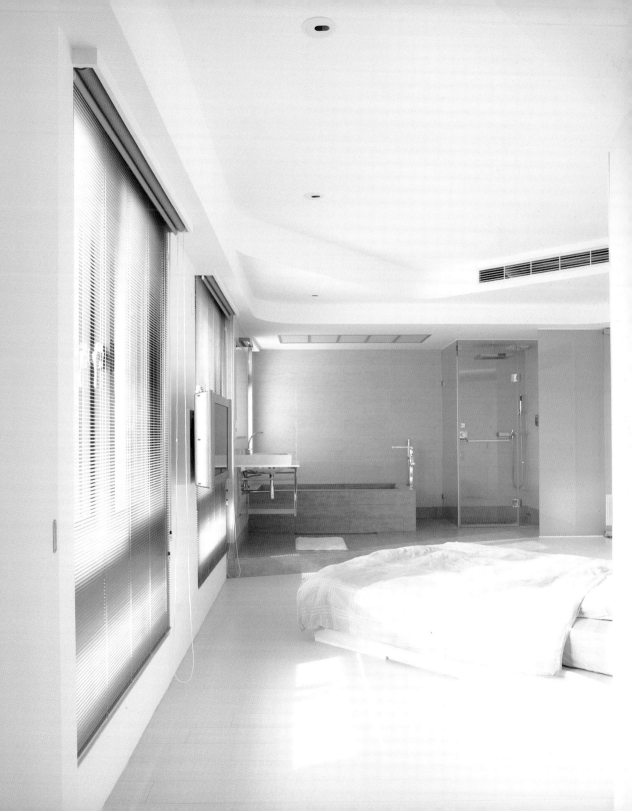

☐ Laura House

Filippo Bombace

After the refurbishment of this apartment, the feature that visually unites all of the spaces is the dark wooden floor. The entrance is separated from the living/dining room by a glass panel. The center of the living room is taken up by a table with a glass top that is lit from above and below. The kitchen is connected to the living area. Behind it is the study, a separate bedroom and a bathroom. The sparse furniture makes the apartment appear larger than it really is. The color scheme is restrained; the dark brown floor and floor-to-ceiling sliding doors create a strong contrast with the white walls and ceilings. Recurring on glass surfaces and objects, blue joins the other two colors to create an effect that is cool and harmonious.

Après la rénovation de cet appartement, le plancher en bois marron foncé est devenu le lien visuel entre toutes les pièces. Un panneau en verre sépare l'entrée de la salle à manger. Au centre du salon se trouve une table dont la surface en verre laisse passer la lumière provenant à la fois d'en haut et d'en bas. La cuisine s'ouvre sur le salon, et derrière elle se trouvent le bureau, la chambre indépendante et une salle de bains. Le mobilier limité confère une impression d'espace au logement. L'appartement présente des couleurs discrètes : le marron foncé du plancher et des portes coulissantes (qui vont du sol au plafond) contraste fortement avec la couleur blanche utilisée pour les murs et les plafonds. Le bleu, que l'on retrouve sur les surfaces vitrées et les objets en verre, s'unit aux deux autres couleurs pour créer une harmonie chromatique offrant une sensation de fraîcheur.

Nach der Renovierung dieses Apartments ist der dunkelbraune Holzfußboden das verbindende Element, das alle Räume visuell zusammenführt. Der Eingang wird vom Wohn- und Essbereich durch eine Glasscheibe abgeschirmt. Den Mittelpunkt des Wohnbereichs bildet ein Tisch mit einer gläsernen Tischplatte, der von oben und unten beleuchtet wird. An den Wohnraum schließt ein Kochbereich an, hinter dem das Arbeitszimmer, der private Schlafbereich und ein Badezimmer liegen. Die sparsame Möblierung lässt die Wohnung größer erscheinen als sie tatsächlich ist. Die Farbgebung des Apartments ist zurückhaltend: Das Dunkelbraun des Fußbodens und der raumhohen Schiebetüren bilden einen starken Kontrast zum Weiß der Wände und Decken. Das in Glasflächen und Glasobjekten immer wiederkehrende Blau verbindet sich mit den beiden anderen Farben zu einem kühl wirkenden Farbakkord.

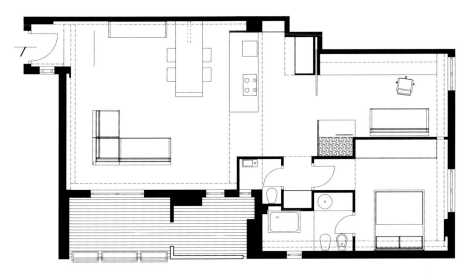

Plan Plan Grundriss

One of the secrets of this apartment is the recurring layers of space – different transparent panels offering interesting perspectives.

L'un des secrets de cet appartement réside dans la présence récurrente de séparations de l'espace : différents panneaux transparents offrent des angles de vue très intéressants.

Ein Geheimnis des Apartments sind die immer wiederkehrenden räumlichen Schichtungen: Unterschiedlich transparente Trennwände ermöglichen interessante Durchblicke.

☐ Space of Femininity

Hank M. Chao

In the design of this apartment for a young woman living on her own, the architects tried to find an expression of space that would do justice to the owner's personality. This small dwelling consists entirely of an entrance, living room, kitchen, bathroom and terrace. The lighting is indirect and comes from light fittings in wall recesses and ceiling moldings. The color scheme is dominated by strong reds and browns that contrast with the soft salmon on walls and ceilings. Passageways, recesses and ceilings are rounded so as not to produce abrupt breaks or throw shadows, and they create pleasant transitions between the rooms in the apartment. The color scheme is also repeated in the different materials and surfaces. The soft materials, such as the fabric in the curtains and the floor coverings, and the hard surfaces, such as enameled elements and the glass mosaic tiles in the bathroom, are color coordinated.

En vue de concevoir un appartement destiné à une jeune femme célibataire, les architectes ont tenté d'élaborer une expression spatiale en harmonie avec le tempérament de la propriétaire. Ce petit logement dispose exclusivement d'une entrée, d'un salon, d'une cuisine, d'une chambre, d'une salle de bains et d'une terrasse. La lumière est obtenue à partir d'un éclairage indirect des niches des murs et des moulures du plafond. La palette de couleurs est dominée par d'intenses tonalités rouges et marron qui contrastent avec la légère couleur saumon des murs et des plafonds. Les zones de passage, les niches et les plafonds présentent des arêtes arrondies qui permettent d'éviter les ombres et les ruptures brutales, en créant des transitions agréables entre les pièces de l'appartement. De plus, on retrouve les mêmes couleurs sur les matériaux et les surfaces les plus divers. Tant les matériaux souples, tels les tissus des rideaux et les tapis, que les surfaces dures, tels les éléments laqués et les mosaïques en verre de la salle de bains, présentent des couleurs assorties.

Bei der Gestaltung des Apartments einer jungen, allein stehenden Frau versuchten die Architekten, einen räumlichen Ausdruck zu finden, der dem Charakter der Bauherrin gerecht wird. Die kleine Wohnung umfasst lediglich Eingangsbereich, Wohnraum, Küche, Schlafzimmer, Badezimmer und Terrasse. Die Lichtstimmung wird durch indirekte Beleuchtung in Wandnischen und Deckenvouten hervorgerufen. Die Farbgestaltung ist von kräftigen Rot- und Brauntönen dominiert, die das zarte Lachsrosa der Wände und Decken kontrastieren. Durchgänge, Nischen und Decken sind abgerundet, um harte Brüche und Schattenwürfe zu vermeiden und angenehme Übergänge zwischen den Räumen des Apartments zu schaffen. Dabei finden sich die gleichen Farben in unterschiedlichsten Materialien und Oberflächen wieder: Weiche Materialien, wie die Stoffe der Vorhänge und Teppiche, und harte Oberflächen, wie lackierte Bauteile und Glasfliesen im Badezimmer, sind farblich aufeinander abgestimmt.

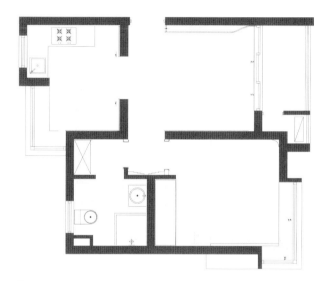

Plan Plan Grundriss

☐ Paderborn Apartment

Christian Schuster

The project for this apartment was modeled on the setting of a James Bond movie. The clean lines of modern architecture are combined with curved and rounded elements to create a world that is inevitably reminiscent of the familiar décor found in sets for 1960s secret-agent movies. For the living space to feel as large as possible, the kitchen, dining and living areas are joined together as a spacious whole. On the other hand, the size of the adjoining rooms and bedroom are reduced to a minimum expression. Certain design features become focal points. There is a spectacular round window set in the curved wall that separates the bedroom from the living area. This window opens like a camera lens shutter. The table in the center has a top that slides over a wall-like console as needed to become a dining table, living room table or kitchen countertop. The color scheme gives a warm and pleasant effect. The recurring use of red combines with other colors and materials to create a homey atmosphere.

L'aménagement de ce petit appartement est inspiré de la scénographie des films de James Bond. Les lignes nettes de l'architecture moderne s'unissent aux éléments ondulés et arrondis, créant une atmosphère qui rappelle les fameux décors des films d'espionnage des années 60. Afin de donner l'impression d'espace maximum, la cuisine, la salle à manger et le salon sont regroupés en une seule unité spatiale ; les pièces secondaires et la chambre affichent, elles, des dimensions réduites. Certains éléments constituent les composantes architecturales les plus importantes. La paroi ondulée qui sépare la chambre comporte une imposante fenêtre circulaire qui s'ouvre tel un obturateur photographique. Le plateau de la table centrale coulisse sur une console en forme de muret, afin qu'en fonction des besoins, celui-ci se transforme en table de salle à manger, de salon ou en plan de travail de cuisine. Les couleurs utilisées génèrent une atmosphère chaleureuse et agréable : le rouge, dominant, offre une ambiance avenante, assortie à différentes couleurs et matériaux.

Für den Entwurf dieses kleinen Apartments stand die Filmarchitektur der James-Bond-Filme Pate: Klare, der Architektur der Moderne verpflichtete Linien verbinden sich mit geschwungenen und abgerundeten Elementen zu einer Formenwelt, die unweigerlich an die berühmten Schauplätze der Agentenfilme der 1960er Jahre erinnert. Um den Wohnraum möglichst groß wirken zu lassen, sind Küche, Ess- und Wohnbereich zu einer räumlichen Einheit zusammengefasst, die Nebenräume und der Schlafraum sind dagegen in ihren Abmessungen minimiert. In einer geschwungenen Wand, die den Schlafraum abtrennt, befindet sich ein spektakuläres, sich ähnlich einer optischen Linse öffnendes, rundes Fenster. Die Platte des zentralen Tischs ist auf einer wandartigen Konsole so verschiebbar, dass sie je nach Bedarf Küchentisch, Esstisch oder Wohnzimmertisch werden kann. Die verwendeten Farben wirken warm und freundlich: Ein immer wiederkehrendes Rot sorgt in Kombination mit unterschiedlichen Farben und Materialien für eine wohnliche Atmosphäre.

Plan Plan Grundriss

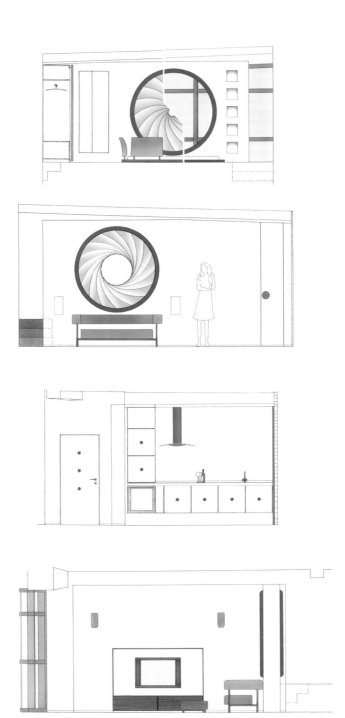

Sections Sections Schnitte

☐ Pier 24 Copenhagen

Kim Utzon Arkitekter

The floor plan of this apartment is a rectangle. The smaller sides are glazed to allow abundant light to enter. The living room occupies one end while the dining room and bedroom are at the opposite end of the dwelling. These areas are separated by an open plan kitchen and bathrooms. The design for this apartment is as a neutral container; a floor of light wood, white walls and concrete ceilings painted white create a spacious and restrained backdrop for a few pieces of valuable, high quality designer furniture, the effect of which is enhanced by their adept arrangement and intense colors. Most of the large pictures are not hung on the wall but simply lean against them. The furniture and pictures do not serve to decorate the apartment but are turned into display pieces.

La surface de cet appartement est rectangulaire, les côtés transversaux sont entièrement vitrés, ce qui permet de faire pénétrer une luminosité abondante à l'intérieur. Le salon se trouve d'un côté de l'habitation, alors que la salle à manger et la chambre se situent à l'autre extrémité. Une cuisine ouverte, située au centre, et les toilettes séparent ces pièces. Le principe formel de ce logement repose sur l'idée d'un conteneur neutre : le plancher en bois clair, les murs blancs et les plafonds en béton peints en blanc offrent un cadre spacieux et discret pour quelques précieux meubles design de grande qualité, dont l'effet est rehaussé par leur distribution astucieuse et leurs couleurs intenses. La plupart des tableaux de grand format sont simplement adossés aux murs au lieu d'y être accrochés. Par conséquent, le mobilier et les tableaux servent non seulement à décorer le logement, mais deviennent aussi des pièces d'exposition.

Die Grundfläche dieses Apartments ist ein Rechteck, dessen Schmalseiten vollständig verglast sind, sodass reichlich Licht ins Innere fällt. Auf der einen Seite befindet sich der Wohnraum; Essraum und Schlafzimmer liegen auf der anderen Seite der Wohnung. Eine zentrale, offene Küche und die Sanitärräume trennen die Bereiche. Das gestalterische Prinzip der Wohnung ist das eines neutralen Containers: Ein heller Holzfußboden, weiße Wände und weiß gestrichene Betondecken schaffen einen großzügigen, unaufdringlichen Hintergrund für einige wenige hochwertige Designermöbel, die durch geschickte Platzierung und ihre kräftigen Farben umso stärkere Wirkung besitzen. Großformatige Bilder hängen zumeist nicht an der Wand, sondern werden einfach angelehnt. Die Möblierung und die Bilder dienen daher nicht nur der Dekoration der Wohnung, sie werden zu Exponaten einer Ausstellung.

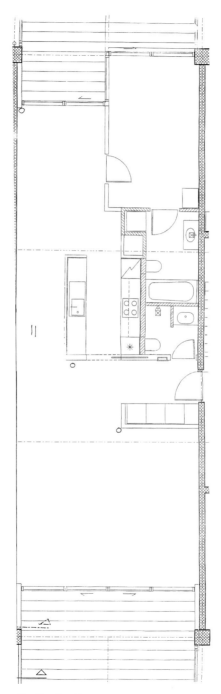

Plan Plan Grundriss

The neutral colors on the walls enhance the effect of the furniture and carefully selected artworks.

Les couleurs neutres des murs permettent d'accentuer l'impression dégagée par les meubles et les œuvres d'art, choisis minutieusement.

Durch die in neutralen Farben gehaltenen Wände wird die Wirkung der sorgfältig ausgesuchten Möbel und Kunstwerke gesteigert.

☐ Fanling Center

Ptang Studio Ltd.

Despite its reduced dimensions, this apartment has all the features of a more spacious dwelling. A small entry area serves as a vestibule for the kitchen and opens onto the living/dining area. Another small stretch of corridor leads from here to the bathroom, finishing at the bedroom and study. The numerous window openings on the three frontages of the dwelling allow natural light into all of the rooms. The furniture is sparse and of an exquisite taste. A meticulous color scheme is the leitmotif of this dwelling. The predominant white base color contrasts with touches of apple green, different woods and bright red. Only the bathroom breaks with the harmonious colors and its large anthracite colored tiles turn it into an independent space.

Malgré sa taille réduite, cet appartement présente toutes les caractéristiques d'une habitation spacieuse : une entrée étroite permet d'accéder à la fois à la cuisine et au salon-salle à manger. Un autre petit tronçon de couloir conduit de celui-ci à la salle de bains, puis à la chambre et au bureau. Les nombreuses fenêtres ouvertes sur les trois façades du logement permettent de faire pénétrer la lumière du jour dans toutes les pièces. Le mobilier est réduit et très raffiné. Une démarche minutieuse sur le choix des couleurs constitue le fil conducteur de cette habitation : le blanc prédomine en tant que couleur de base et contraste avec des touches vert pomme, des tons couleur bois et un rouge intense. Seule la salle de bains, dont le sol et les murs sont recouverts de grands carreaux aux tons anthracite, rompt l'harmonie chromatique, devenant ainsi un espace indépendant.

Das Apartment verfügt trotz seiner geringen Größe über alle Attribute einer geräumigen Wohnung: Ein schmaler Eingangsbereich dient zugleich als Vorraum der Küche und führt in den Wohn- und Essraum. Ein weiterer kleiner Flurbereich leitet von diesem zum Bad und schließlich zum Schlaf- und Arbeitszimmer über. Die vielen Fenster auf drei Seiten der Wohnung ermöglichen in allen Räumen natürliches Tageslicht. Die Möblierung ist sparsam und von exquisitem Geschmack. Ein durchdachtes Farbkonzept ist der gestalterische Leitfaden durch diese Wohnung: Die vorherrschende weiße Grundfarbe wird durch apfelgrüne, holzfarbene und kräftige rote Akzente kontrastiert. Lediglich das Badezimmer, dessen Fußboden und Wände mit großformatigen, anthrazitfarbenen Fliesen verkleidet sind, bricht mit der Farbharmonie und wird somit zu einem eigenständigen, besonderen Ort.

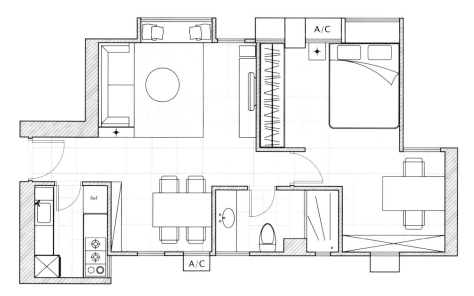

Plan Plan Grundriss

The small bathroom is turned into a special place through its precision design. The large mirrored surfaces visually enlarge the room.

La petite salle de bains devient un espace singulier grâce à son design précis. Les grands miroirs offrent l'illusion d'un espace agrandi.

Das kleine Badezimmer wird durch seine präzise Detaillierung zu einem besonderen Ort. Große Spiegelflächen vergrößern optisch den Raum.

Apartment in Cannes Garden

Gary Chang, Raymond Chan/EDGE (HK) Ltd.

The core of this project is the conversion of an unused bedroom into a multi-functional space. In order to give this flexibility of use to the study and to connect the other rooms of the apartment depending on need, the architects designed a pivoting wall unit. When it is opened, additional space is merged directly into the living room. A passageway joins the living-room with the main bedroom and the study, and different spatial layouts become possible. When the wall unit is closed, the dwelling goes back to being a conventional three-bedroom apartment. The great effect produced by the movement of the room divider is enhanced by the strong contrast of the light and dark colors of the materials. The contrast between the dark wood of the furniture and the white walls seems to break down the coherence of the space.

Ce projet a pour principal objectif de transformer une chambre inutile en une pièce à usages multiples. Afin de pouvoir utiliser ce bureau de manière flexible et relier les autres pièces du logement en fonction des besoins, les architectes ont conçu une cloison pivotante qui sert également d'armoire : lorsqu'on l'ouvre on obtient un espace supplémentaire qui conduit directement au salon. Un couloir relie le salon à la chambre principale et au bureau, et les pièces peuvent être agencées entre elles de différentes manières. À l'inverse, lorsque la cloison pivotante est fermée, le logement redevient un trois-pièces conventionnel. L'effet provoqué par le déplacement de cette pièce mobile au niveau de l'espace est accentué par l'intense clair-obscur des matériaux : le contraste entre le bois sombre des meubles et les murs blancs semble bouleverser l'équilibre spatial.

Das Kernstück des Projekts ist die Umwandlung eines nicht benötigten Schlafraums in ein Mehrzweckzimmer. Um diesen Arbeitsraum flexibel nutzbar zu machen und den anderen Räumen der Wohnung bei Bedarf zuschalten zu können, entwarfen die Architekten einen drehbaren Wandschrank: Ist dieser geöffnet, entsteht ein zusätzlicher Raum, der direkt in das Wohnzimmer übergeht. Ein Flur verbindet den Wohnbereich mit Elternschlafzimmer und Arbeitsraum, und neue Relationen der Räume untereinander werden möglich. Wenn der Wandschrank dagegen geschlossen ist, verwandelt sich die Wohnung wieder in eine konventionelle Dreizimmerwohnung. Der effektvolle Umgang mit dem beweglichen Raumteiler wird durch starke Hell-Dunkel-Kontraste bei der Materialisierung unterstrichen: Der Kontrast zwischen dem dunklen Holz der Möbel und den weißen Wänden scheint den Raumzusammenhang aufzulösen.

Apartment in Brasilia

Fernandes Capanema Arquitetura

At the time this two-story dwelling was being refurbished, the owner especially wanted it to become an oasis for rest and relaxation. The existing layout – small bedrooms, a very large staircase and many dark elements – was replaced with a bright, open and light design. The continuous space connecting the living-dining area and kitchen is the core of the dwelling. Large sliding doors hide the kitchen from being seen by visitors. A light, filigree spiral staircase leads to the upper floor where the sleeping area, bathroom, dressing room and study are located. Glass walls and mirrors create subtle divisions of space inside the dwelling. The warm artificial lighting creates a contrast with the predominantly pale and cold color of the walls, ceilings and built-in elements.

Lors de la rénovation de ce logement de deux étages, le proprié-taire souhaitait tout particulièrement créer un havre de paix et de détente. L'ancienne distribution du logement (petites chambres, escalier trop grand et nombreux éléments sombres) a été modifiée pour obtenir un espace plus lumineux, plus ouvert et plus léger. L'espace continu qui relie le salon, la salle à manger et la cuisine constitue le cœur de l'habitation. De grandes portes coulissantes permettent de dissimuler la cuisine au regard des invités. Un petit escalier en colimaçon, tout en filigrane, conduit à l'étage supérieur, où se trouvent la chambre, la salle de bains, le dressing et le bureau. Les cloisons en verre et les miroirs créent de subtiles séparations à l'intérieur du logement. La lumière artificielle chaude contraste avec les tons dominants clairs et froids des murs, des plafonds et des éléments encastrés.

Beim Umbau dieser zweigeschossigen Wohnung legte der Bau-herr besonderen Wert darauf, eine Oase der Ruhe und Entspan-nung zu schaffen. Die bestehende Ausstattung der Wohnung – kleine Räume, eine viel zu große Treppe und viele dunkle Ele-mente – wurde durch ein helles, offenes und leicht wirkendes Design ersetzt. Der ineinander übergehende, offene Wohn-, Ess- und Küchenbereich ist das Zentrum der Wohnung. Große Schie-betüren verbergen die Küche vor den Augen der Besucher. Eine leichte, filigran wirkende Spindeltreppe führt ins Obergeschoss, wo sich Schlafraum, Bad, Ankleide- und Arbeitsbereich befinden. Glaswände und Spiegel schaffen subtile Trennungen innerhalb der Wohnung. Warmes Kunstlicht bildet einen Kontrast zu den vorwiegend kalten, hellen Farbtönen der Wände, Decken und Einbauten.

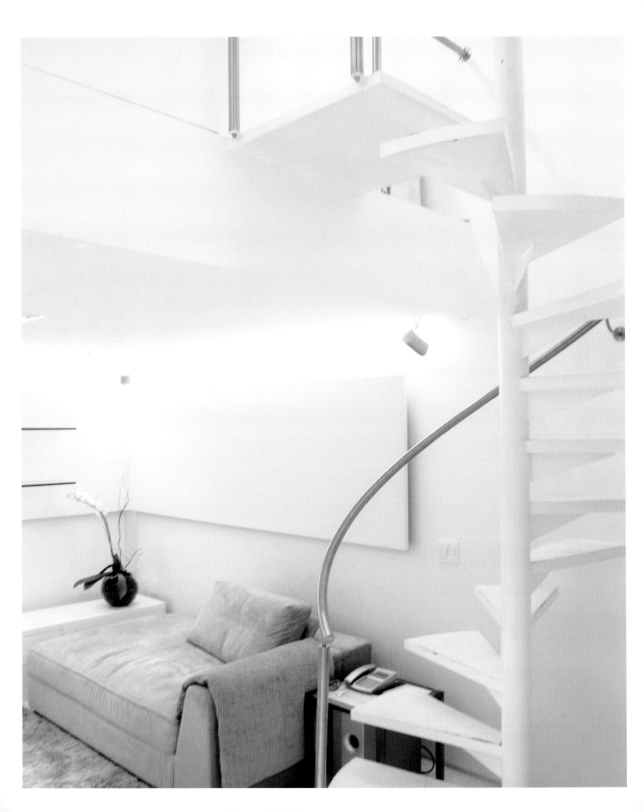

A light, white-enameled spiral staircase connects the lower level living area with the upper floor sleeping area.

Un escalier en colimaçon laqué blanc de style aérien relie le salon du niveau inférieur à la chambre de l'étage supérieur.

Eine leicht wirkende, weiß lackierte Spindeltreppe verbindet die unten gelegene Wohnebene mit der oberen Schlafebene.

☐ Origami House

García y Ruiz Arquitectos

This dwelling is a prototype apartment belonging to an appliance manufacturer. In order to make this reduced space seem larger, it was divided by means of a diagonal structure with multiple folds. The architects were inspired by origami, the Japanese art of paper-folding, to create this three-dimensional form with a dynamic effect. The center of the apartment is the kitchen/living area, located on the middle level. Here the latest in home automation is presented. The appliances are integrated in the design in such a way that they seem to be part of the walls. Comfort and simplicity of use are foremost. The private spaces, such as the bathroom and bedroom, are hidden behind the folded structure, unlike the completely open living room. The whole dwelling has been kept a bright white. The light color scheme makes the apartment seem larger.

Cette habitation est un « appartement témoin » utilisé par un fabricant d'électroménager. Afin de donner de l'ampleur à cet espace réduit, le volume a été divisé selon une structure diagonale à plusieurs plis. Les architectes se sont inspirés de la technique japonaise de l'origami pour créer cette structure tridimensionnelle à effet dynamique. La cuisine-salle à manger, située à l'étage intermédiaire, constitue l'élément central du logement. Celle-ci est équipée des toutes dernières nouveautés en domotique. Les appareils électroménagers sont si bien intégrés au design qu'ils semblent faire partie intégrante des murs. L'habitabilité et la simplicité d'utilisation constituent les caractéristiques essentielles du logement. Les pièces les plus intimes, telles que la salle de bains et la chambre, sont dissimulées derrière la structure pliable alors que le salon, au contraire, s'ouvre amplement. L'ensemble du logement affiche un blanc lumineux. La couleur claire offre une impression d'espace au logement.

Bei dieser Wohnung handelt es sich um die Musterwohnung eines Herstellers von Haushaltsgeräten. Um den beschränkten Raum größer erscheinen zu lassen, ist das Volumen durch eine diagonal verlaufende, mehrfach gefaltete Struktur gegliedert. Für diese dynamisch wirkende, dreidimensionale Form ließen sich die Architekten durch japanische Origami-Falttechniken inspirieren. Das Zentrum der Wohnung bildet die Wohnküche, die sich auf der mittleren Ebene befindet. Hier wird der neueste Stand der Haushaltstechnik in der Praxis präsentiert. Dabei sind die Haushaltsgeräte so in das Design integriert, dass sie wie den Wänden zugehörig erscheinen. Dabei steht die Wohnlichkeit und die Gebrauchsfreundlichkeit im Vordergrund. Die privateren Räume, wie Badezimmer und Schlafraum, werden von der gefalteten Struktur verborgen, der Wohnraum dagegen öffnet sich weit. Die gesamte Wohnung ist in leuchtendem Weiß gehalten. Die helle Farbstimmung lässt die Wohnung größer wirken.

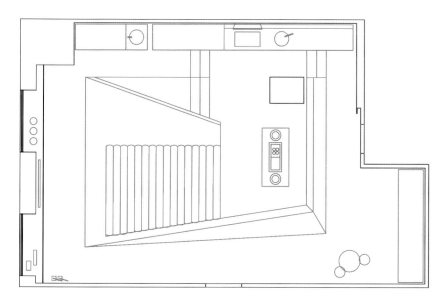

Plan Plan Grundriss

The folding structure creates an expressive and dynamic effect. The contrast with the raw frame of the building around it is intentional.

La structure pliable produit un effet expressif et dynamique. Le contraste avec la structure portante à l'état brut du bâtiment qui l'entoure est délibéré.

Die gefaltete Struktur wirkt expressiv und dynamisch. Der Kontrast zur rohen Tragstruktur des umgebenden Gebäudes ist beabsichtigt.

☐ Gramercy Park Apartment

Page Goolrick Architect PC

The objective of the architects in refurbishing this small loft, previously without any internal divisions, was to maintain the ampleness of the space while adapting it to the specific requirements of the owners. The first step was to move the kitchen, which had been located against the outer wall, to an open area directly connected to the living-dining room. The architects placed the bedroom in the space occupied by the kitchen, which receives light through the old kitchen window. If required, it can be closed off by means of sliding glass panels, some of which are opal glass while others are opaque. When the panels are retracted, the resulting living area is ample and open. A number of large built-in closets guarantee that the apartment looks ordered and spacious, despite its limited size. The entire apartment is decorated in pale colors, particularly white and beige, while the floor is dark parquet. The furniture keeps to the same color scheme.

Lors de la rénovation de ce petit loft, qui auparavant ne présentait aucune séparation intérieure, les architectes se sont fixé pour objectif de conserver l'ample espace disponible, en l'adaptant aux souhaits spécifiques des propriétaires. Une première étape a consisté à déplacer la cuisine, située auparavant au niveau du mur extérieur, vers une pièce ouverte, qui communique directement avec la salle à manger. À sa place, les architectes ont installé la chambre, qui est éclairée par l'ancienne fenêtre de la cuisine et peut être séparée, si on le souhaite, à l'aide de panneaux coulissants. Lorsque les cloisons sont ouvertes, l'espace semble plus ample et offre une plus grande ouverture. Malgré ses dimensions réduites, le logement semble ordonné et spacieux grâce aux possibilités de rangement offertes par de grands placards. L'appartement est décoré dans son ensemble avec des couleurs claires, parmi lesquelles prédominent le blanc et le beige. Le sol est en parquet sombre et le mobilier reste dans la même gamme chromatique.

Beim Umbau dieses kleinen Lofts, das zuvor keine Aufteilung in einzelne Räume aufwies, versuchten die Architekten, die räumliche Großzügigkeit zu bewahren, es jedoch den spezifischen Wünschen der Bauherren anzupassen. Als erster Schritt wurde die vorher an der Außenwand gelegene Küche in eine offene Nische mit direktem Kontakt zum Wohn- und Essbereich verlegt. An ihre Stelle platzierten die Architekten den Schlafraum, der durch das ehemalige Küchenfenster belichtet wird und durch Schiebewände, teils aus Milchglas, teils undurchsichtig, bei Bedarf abtrennbar ist. Bei geöffneten Schiebewänden wirkt der entstehende Wohnbereich großzügig und offen. Große Wandschränke sorgen dafür, dass die Wohnung trotz ihrer beschränkten Größe aufgeräumt und geräumig wirkt. Die gesamte Wohnung ist in hellen Farbtönen gehalten, wobei Weiß und Beige vorherrschen. Der Fußboden besteht aus dunklem Holzparkett. Die Möblierung ist im selben Farbspektrum gehalten.

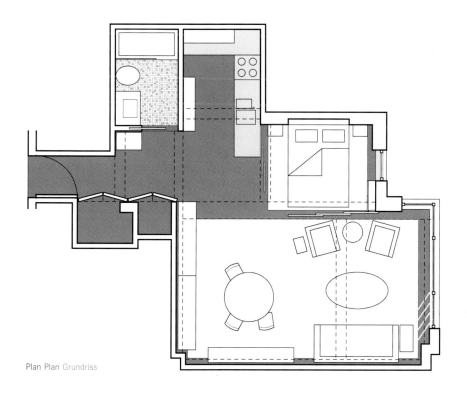

Plan Plan Grundriss

The kitchen is hidden in a space of the apartment without windows, but as a result of its well thought out design and openness, it is still an appealing space.

La cuisine a été dissimulée dans un espace sans fenêtre, mais grâce à sa distribution judicieuse et son ouverture, cette pièce conserve tout son attrait.

Die Küche ist zwar in eine fensterlose Nische der Wohnung gerückt worden; durch ihre durchdachte Aufteilung und ihre Offenheit ist sie dennoch ein attraktiver Raum.

de Kooning
TADAO ANDO LIGHT AND WATER
Construction
Andy Goldsworthy HAND TO EARTH
Berthold LUBETKIN
JACOBSEN
CITY HOME
Le Corbusier

☐ **Villa Slit**

C. Matsuda / Tele-design

Living in a reduced space is anything but unusual in Japan. This house, which only covers 722 sq ft of habitable space, is located in a densely built-up residential area of Tokyo. The kitchen and dining room are found on the first floor. A steep and narrow staircase leads to the living room on the second floor. The bedroom and a terrace have been laid out above this. The façade is covered with a system of bamboo window shades that constantly change the visual effect whenever they are unrolled. The interior also makes use of bamboo blinds, which allow spaces to be defined and extended with their ever-changing transparency. Consequently, the style of this dwelling is not traditional but modern, and it contains valuable minimalist details. Predominant use has been made of natural materials like wood and wicker.

Au Japon, vivre dans un espace réduit n'est pas quelque chose d'inhabituel. Cette maison, de seulement 67 m² de surface habitable, a été construite dans une zone résidentielle très urbanisée de Tokyo. La cuisine et la salle à manger se trouvent au rez-de-chaussée. On accède au salon, situé au premier étage, par un escalier raide et étroit. Au-dessus ont été installées la chambre et une terrasse. La façade est couverte d'un système de persiennes en bambou qui, une fois déroulées, modifient constamment l'effet visuel. L'intérieur est également doté de persiennes en bambou qui, grâce à leur transparence variable, permettent de délimiter les espaces et de les agrandir visuellement. Par conséquent, la décoration de ce logement n'est pas traditionnelle mais plutôt moderne, avec de précieux détails minimalistes. Les matériaux utilisés sont essentiellement naturels, tels que le bois et l'osier.

In Japan ist es alles andere als ungewöhnlich, auf engstem Raum zu leben. Dieses Haus, das nur 67 m² Wohnfläche umfasst, wurde in einem dicht bebauten Wohngebiet von Tokio errichtet. Im Erdgeschoss befinden sich Küche und Essraum. Über eine steile, enge Treppe erreicht man den Wohnraum in der ersten Etage. Darüber angeordnet sind der Schlafraum und eine Terrasse. Die Fassade wird durch ein System von Bambusrollos bedeckt, durch deren Aufrollen ein konstanter Wechsel des optischen Eindrucks entsteht. Bambusrollos finden sich auch im Inneren, wo sie mit ihrer sich verändernden Transparenz Bereiche abgrenzen und optisch erweitern können. Dabei ist die Gestaltung der Wohnung nicht traditionell, sondern konsequent modern mit minimalistischer, hochwertiger Detaillierung. Es wurden überwiegend natürliche Materialien wie Holz und Korbgeflecht verwendet.

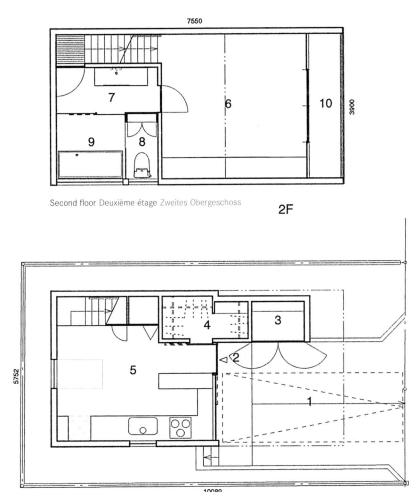

7550

3900

7

9   8

6

10

Second floor Deuxième étage Zweites Obergeschoss   2F

5752

5

4   3

2

1

10080

First floor Premier étage Erstes Obergeschoss

103

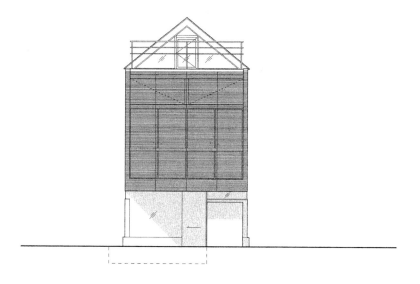

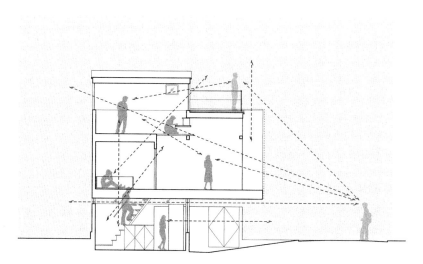

Sections Sections Schnitte

☐ Apartment K

Atelier Peter Ebner - Franziska Ullmann

This small apartment in a 1950s lakeside building is a vacation home for a family of five. Owing to its small surface area, it was more convenient to maintain the large, multi-purpose room instead of converting it into small single-function rooms. An inbuilt closet and a floor-to-ceiling central unit form the core of this new layout. Hiding behind sliding partitions and folding doors there are multiple shelves, light fittings, pull-out tables and even a small bathroom. By changing the position of movable elements, new combinations can be created to allow the space to be used in a variety of ways. This allows full use to be made of the rooms so that there is always enough space for the family. The floor, walls and ceiling are covered with leaf and branch motifs painted by an artist.

Cette petite habitation, logée dans un bâtiment construit près d'un lac vers 1950, devait être transformée en maison de vacances pour une famille de cinq personnes. Étant donné sa surface réduite, il était préférable de conserver la grande salle relativement flexible, plutôt que de la séparer en petites pièces monofonctionnelles. Un placard et un meuble central, allant du sol au plafond, constituent le cœur de cette nouvelle distribution de l'espace. Des cloisons coulissantes et des portes battantes et pliantes cachent de nombreuses étagères, éléments d'éclairage, tables amovibles et même un coin toilettes. En changeant la position des éléments mobiles on peut créer de nouvelles combinaisons permettant d'utiliser l'espace de différentes manières. Les pièces sont donc parfaitement exploitées de façon à ce qu'il y ait toujours suffisamment de place pour toute la famille. Un motif de feuilles et de branches a été peint par un artiste sur le plancher, les murs et le plafond.

Die kleine Wohnung in einem um 1950 an einem See erbauten Haus sollte zu einer Ferienwohnung für eine fünfköpfige Familie umgebaut werden. Aufgrund der kleinen Grundfläche lag es nahe, den großen, flexibel nutzbaren Raum möglichst zu erhalten und nicht in kleine, monofunktionale Räume umzubauen. Herzstücke der neuen Aufteilung sind ein zentral im Raum platziertes, raumhohes Möbel und eine Schrankwand. Hinter Schiebewänden, Klapp- und Falttüren befinden sich eine Vielzahl von Staufächern und Beleuchtungselementen sowie ausziehbare Betten und sogar ein Sanitärbereich. Durch Verschieben der beweglichen Elemente zu immer neuen Kombinationen ergeben sich vielfältige Nutzungsmöglichkeiten. Der zur Verfügung stehende Raum wird so optimal ausgenutzt und bietet der gesamten Familie jederzeit ausreichend Platz. Boden, Wand und Decke wurden von einem Künstler mit einem Muster aus Blättern und Zweigen bemalt.

10m 5m 1m

The positioning of free-standing furniture left enough space to include a children's room. The bathroom is simple and functional.

Grâce à la distribution des meubles, il reste suffisamment d'espace pour ajouter une chambre d'enfants. La salle de bains est simple et fonctionnelle.

Durch das frei in den Raum gestellte Möbel bleibt genügend Platz für ein Kinderzimmer. Das Badezimmer ist schlicht und funktional.

☐ "Vivo sola y me mola"

Pablo Fernández Lorenzo & Pablo Redondo Díez

The L-shaped dwelling, lying between the street and a courtyard, is structured around three free-standing stainless steel kitchen units in a line continuing to include a free-standing, completely glassed-in shower. This line is flanked by a large built-in closet on one side, inside which there are kitchen cabinets, shelves and a small toilet. While the kitchen unit can be extended with a table that slides towards the living room, at the other end, in the direction of the bedroom, the shower can be separated by means of sliding doors. This brilliant system gives the apartment spatial versatility and variety, despite its narrow shape. The use of materials and color is totally minimalist. All of the built-in furniture and the walls are bright white; the only different touches come from the stainless steel and glass.

Le logement qui s'étend en forme de L entre une rue et une cour intérieure, présente une structure composée de trois meubles de cuisine en acier inoxydable, prolongée d'une cabine de douche entièrement vitrée et également indépendante. Sur un côté de ce segment est installé un long placard, où viennent se loger les meubles de cuisine, des étagères et une petite salle d'eau. De même que le meuble de cuisine peut être prolongé vers le salon grâce à une table à rallonge, à l'autre extrémité, en allant vers la chambre, la douche peut être séparée grâce à des portes coulissantes. Malgré son exiguïté, l'appartement offre une grande flexibilité et diversité grâce à cette structure ingénieuse. L'emploi des matériaux et de la couleur est totalement minimaliste. Tous les placards et les murs sont d'un blanc éclatant et seuls l'acier inoxydable et le verre apportent une touche différente.

Die im Grundriss L-förmige Wohnung, die zwischen einer Straße und einem Innenhof liegt, wird durch frei im Raum stehende Küchenmöbel aus Edelstahl strukturiert, fortgeführt ebenfalls in einer freistehenden, rundum verglasten Dusche. Ein langer Einbauschrank flankiert diesen Tresen auf der einen Seite und nimmt Küchenschränke, Abstellflächen und einen kleinen Toilettenbereich auf. Während das Küchenmöbel zum Wohnraum hin durch einen ausfahrbaren Esstisch erweitert werden kann, ist es am anderen Ende, in Richtung des Schlafbereichs, möglich, die Dusche durch Schiebetüren abzuteilen. Durch den genialen Kunstgriff besitzt die Wohnung trotz ihrer Enge eine räumliche Flexibilität und Vielfalt. Die Verwendung von Materialien und Farbe ist dabei minimalistisch. Alle Einbaumöbel und Wände sind in strahlendem Weiß gehalten, lediglich Edelstahl und Glas setzen besondere Akzente.

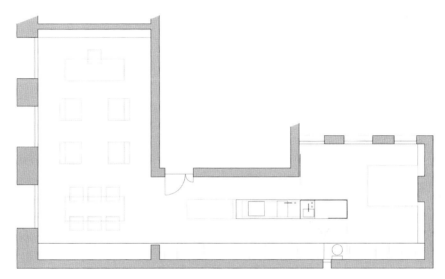

Plan Plan Grundriss

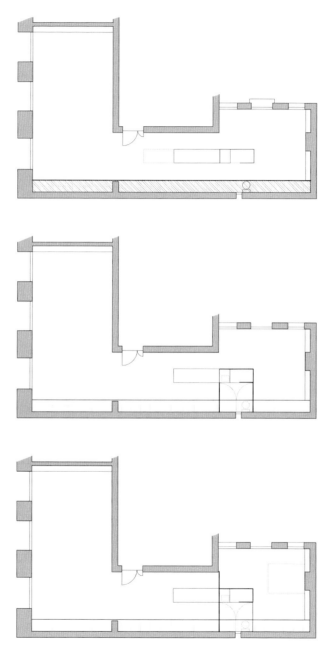

Bathroom enclosure Fermeture de la salle de bains Badezimmerumschließung

☐ Apartment of Ben Haitsma

Ben Haitsma

A large number of refined details make this small attic into a practical and comfortable apartment where you forget the limitations of space. The useful surfaces are limited by the slope of the roof, but the light walls in different materials and shades reflect the plentiful natural light entering to make the spaces look bigger than they really are. The many corners and nooks in the apartment are taken advantage of with custom-made built-in furniture. The furniture is also in light shades that contrast with the dark parquet floor. The highlight of the apartment is the bathroom. It is paved in natural stone and glass mosaic tiles that produce an effect of openness thanks to the windows and the large mirrored surface.

Un grand nombre de détails raffinés font de ce petit appartement sur les toits un logement pratique et commode qui fait oublier les inconvénients d'un espace réduit. Les surfaces utiles sont limitées par les inclinaisons du plafond, mais les murs clairs de différents matériaux et tonalités reflètent la lumière du jour, qui pénètre en abondance, conférant aux pièces une sensation d'espace agrandi. On a tiré profit des nombreux angles et recoins de l'habitation pour encastrer des meubles fabriqués sur mesure. Le mobilier présente également des tons clairs qui contrastent avec le parquet en bois sombre. Le joyau de cet appartement est certainement la salle de bains, dont le revêtement en pierre naturelle et mosaïques de verre produit une sensation d'ouverture et de luminosité par le biais de fenêtres et de miroirs de grande taille.

Eine Fülle raffinierter Details macht diese kleine Dachwohnung zu einer praktischen, komfortablen Wohnung, die die räumlichen Beschränkungen vergessen lässt. Durch die Dachschrägen sind die nutzbaren Flächen reduziert, doch die hellen Wände in unterschiedlichen Materialien und Farbtönen reflektieren das reichlich einfallende Tageslicht und lassen die Räume dadurch größer erscheinen, als sie tatsächlich sind. Die vielen Winkel und Ecken der Wohnung werden durch maßgefertigte Einbaumöbel ausgenutzt. Auch das Mobiliar ist in hellen Farbtönen gehalten und kontrastiert auf diese Weise mit dem Parkettfußboden aus dunklem Holz. Ein besonderer Höhepunkt der Wohnung ist das mit Glasfliesen und Naturstein ausgekleidete Bad, das durch große Spiegelflächen und Fenster ebenfalls offen und hell wirkt.

The effective details and suitable color scheme make this a homey apartment, despite its small size.
Les détails efficaces et une couleur très soignée font de cette habitation une maison accueillante, malgré son espace réduit.
Effektvolle Details und ein durchdachtes Farbkonzept machen die Wohnung trotz ihrer geringen Größe zu einem wohnlichen Zuhause.

Greenwich Village Condominium

CCS Architecture

The refurbishment of this small apartment, consisting only of a living-dining room, placed priority on the inclusion of a separate bedroom and additional storage space. The bedroom is located in the space previously occupied by a walk-in closet. It fulfills all of the conditions for a bedroom – there is a bed with a spacious storage drawer and a shelf for books, magazines and lamps. A small window in the curved wall allows the view from the living room windows to be seen from the bed. The living room is furnished with a centrally positioned table and a sofa. The long walls are lined with large floor to ceiling built-in closets. Mirrored walls make this small apartment seem bigger.

La rénovation de ce petit appartement, uniquement constitué d'un salon-salle à manger, avait pour priorité d'ajouter une chambre à part et des espaces de rangement supplémentaires. La chambre se situe dans l'espace auparavant occupé par un dressing et est séparée du salon par une cloison courbe qui n'arrive pas jusqu'au plafond. Elle dispose de toutes les commodités nécessaires : un lit placé sur un tiroir spacieux et une étagère pour livres, revues et lampes. Une petite fenêtre ouverte dans la cloison courbe permet d'apercevoir les baies vitrées du salon depuis le lit. Le salon est meublé d'une table, située au milieu, et d'un canapé. Les murs longitudinaux présentent de grands placards encastrés allant du sol jusqu'au plafond. La surface réfléchissante des murs offre une impression d'espace.

Im Vordergrund des Umbaus dieses kleinen, nur aus einem einzigen Wohn- und Essraum bestehenden Apartments stand die Integration eines separaten Schlafzimmers und zusätzlicher Abstellflächen. Der Schlafraum wurde auf der Grundfläche eines ehemaligen Ankleidezimmers eingerichtet und ist vom Wohnraum durch eine nicht ganz bis zur Decke geführte, gebogene Wand abgetrennt. Es enthält alle Requisiten eines Schlafzimmers: Ein Bett mit einem geräumigen Bettkasten sowie ein Regalbrett für Bücher, Zeitschriften und Lampen. Ein kleines Sichtfenster in der gebogenen Wand ermöglicht den Blick vom Bett bis hin zu den Fenstern des Wohnraums. Das Wohnzimmer selbst ist mit einem zentral positionierten Tisch und einem Sofa möbliert. Große, bis zur Decke reichende Wandschränke säumen beide Längsseiten. Verspiegelte Wände lassen die kleine Wohnung größer erscheinen.

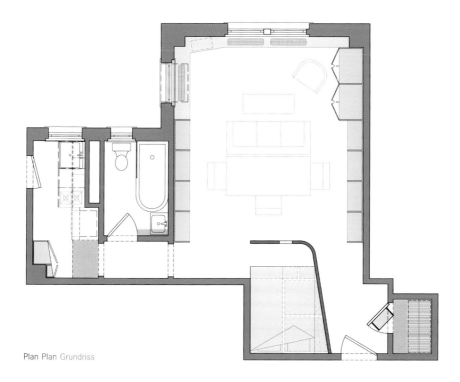

Plan Plan Grundriss

☐ ER Apartment

Francesc Rifé

This apartment belongs to a chocolate maker and is located above his business. It is made up of a dwelling and studio, separated from the rest of the residence by the bathroom suite. The kitchen is inside a closet. When this built-in unit is closed, the kitchen is hidden from the view of guests. In the living room, an opaque glass sliding door separates a raised sleeping area from the rest of the room. The floors are of wood with a natural finish; the walls and floors are either enameled or painted in white. All of the built-in furniture is designed to merge with the walls. A large desk is the focal point of the spacious study, while a built-in cabinet serves as a display case for the different chocolate products. The two areas of the apartment are lighted with recessed halogen spotlights.

Cet appartement appartient à un chocolatier et se trouve au-dessus de son commerce. Il est composé d'un logement et d'un bureau séparés du reste de l'habitation par la zone de toilette. La cuisine est intégrée à une armoire murale. Lorsque l'on ferme ce meuble encastré, la cuisine devient invisible pour les invités. Dans le salon, une porte coulissante en verre opaque permet d'isoler un espace surélevé où se trouve la chambre. Les sols sont en bois avec finition naturelle ; les murs et les plafonds sont laqués ou peints en blanc. Tous les meubles encastrés ont été conçus de sorte qu'ils se fondent dans les murs en formant un tout. Un grand plan de travail constitue le cœur de cette spa-cieuse salle de travail et une armoire murale tient lieu de présen-toir des différents produits de ce chocolatier. Les deux pièces de l'appartement sont éclairées par des spots intégrés au plafond.

Das Apartment eines Schokoladenherstellers befindet sich über seinem Geschäft. Es umfasst einen Wohnbereich sowie ein Stu-dio, das durch einen Sanitärblock vom Rest der Wohnung getrennt ist. Der Küchenbereich ist Teil einer Schrankwand. Schließt man dieses Einbaumöbel, bleibt die Küche den Blicken der Gäste verborgen. Im Wohnbereich trennt eine Schiebetür aus undurchsichtigem Glas eine erhöht gelegene Schlafnische vom Rest des Raumes ab. Für die Fußböden wurde naturbelassenes Holz verwendet, Wände und Decken sind weiß lackiert oder gestrichen. Alle Einbaumöbel sind so gestaltet, dass sie mit den Wänden zu einer Einheit verschmelzen. Den Mittelpunkt des groß-zügigen Studios bildet ein großer Arbeitstisch; eine Schrankwand dient als Ausstellungsfläche für die unterschiedlichen Produkte des Schokoladenherstellers. Beide Bereiche des Apartments wer-den durch in die Decke integrierte Einbaustrahler beleuchtet.

Plan Plan Grundriss

Separated by a sliding opaque glass panel, the sleeping area is severe and Spartan.

La chambre, séparée par une cloison coulissante en verre opaque, dégage une austérité spartiate.

Die durch eine undurchsichtige Schiebewand aus Glas abgetrennte Schlafnische ist von spartanisch wirkender Kargheit.

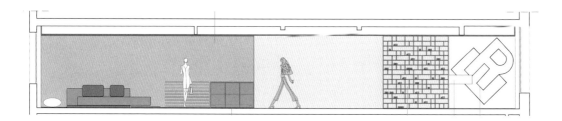

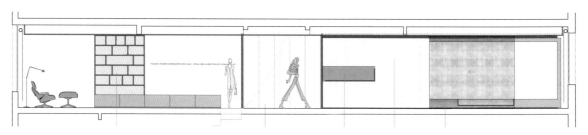

Sections Sections Schnitte

□ Apartment on Rue St. Fiacre

Philippe Harden & Atelier 9 Portes

The refurbishment of this small two-room central Paris apartment had the aim of making full use of the limited space. The suspended ceiling was removed to give a room height of 10 ft. The largest room was turned into a living room containing an open kitchen with an island in the center. The adjoining dining area is spacious with natural lighting. The living room and bedroom are separated by a core that includes a bathroom and walk-in wardrobe. The shelving unit running the length of the apartment along the passageway is a unifying feature. The walls and ceiling of the apartment are mainly white; only a few elements, such as a wall recess, the countertops in the kitchen and the central core are in dark, anthracite and brown shades. The floor is paved in traditional, irregular terracotta tiles.

La rénovation de ce petit logement de deux pièces, situé au cœur de Paris, avait pour but de tirer parti au maximum du peu d'espace disponible. Le faux-plafond existant a été retiré afin d'obtenir une hauteur de 3 mètres à l'intérieur. La plus grande pièce a été transformée en salon, au milieu duquel se trouve le module de cuisine indépendante. La salle à manger attenante est spacieuse et bénéficie d'un éclairage naturel. Le salon et la chambre sont séparés par une zone de toilette, qui comprend une salle de bains et un dressing. L'étagère qui s'étend le long du couloir, et tout le long du logement, constitue un élément unificateur. La plupart des murs et des plafonds de l'appartement sont blancs ; seuls certains éléments, tels qu'une niche, le plan de travail de la cuisine ou encore l'espace central occupé par la zone de toilette, présentent des tonalités sombres (anthracite et marron). Le plancher est recouvert d'un carrelage traditionnel et irrégulier en terre cuite.

Durch die Renovierung dieser kleinen Zweizimmerwohnung im Zentrum von Paris sollte der beschränkte Raum bestmöglich ausgenutzt werden. Die bestehende abgehängte Decke wurde entfernt, um eine Deckenhöhe von 3 m zu erzielen. Der größte Raum wurde zu einem Wohnraum mit offener Küche umgestaltet, in dessen Zentrum sich ein frei stehender Küchenblock befindet. Der angrenzende Essbereich ist großzügig gestaltet und natürlich belichtet. Ein Sanitärkern, der Badezimmer und Ankleidebereich aufnimmt, trennt den Wohn- vom Schlafraum. Ein über die ganze Länge der Wohnung verlaufendes Wandregal formt entlang des entstehenden Korridors ein verbindendes Element. Die Wände und Decken der Wohnung sind überwiegend weiß, lediglich einige wenige Elemente, wie eine Nische und die Arbeitsfläche in der Küche und der zentrale Sanitärkern, sind in dunklen Anthrazit- und Brauntönen gehalten. Der Boden besteht aus traditionellen, unregelmäßigen Terrakottafliesen.

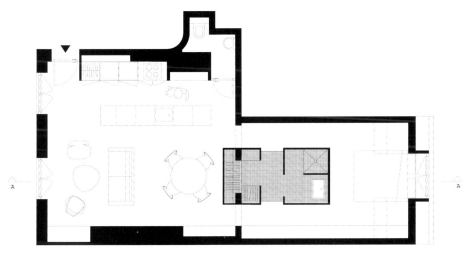

Plan Plan Grundriss

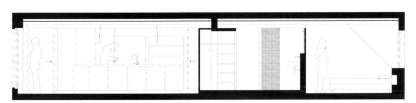

Section Section Schnitt

The walls of the core containing the walk-in wardrobe and bathroom do not reach the raw concrete ceiling, which contrasts with the delicate details of the bathroom.

Les murs de la zone de toilette, qui comprend le dressing et la salle de bains, n'arrivent pas jusqu'au plafond en béton brut, ce qui contraste avec les détails raffinés de la salle de bains.

Die Wände des Sanitärbereichs, welcher Ankleide und Bad umfasst, reichen nicht bis zur rohen Betondecke. Diese kontrastiert die feine Detaillierung des Badezimmers.

☐ Piazza Biancamano

Elena Sacco & Paolo Danelli/DAP Studio

This 14th-floor apartment in a Milan high-rise was designed with the idea of continuous, flowing space. The rooms are laid out in such a way that the common areas of the dwelling connect with the private quarters without any barriers, such as walls or closed doors, breaking this continuity. An independent kitchen module serves to structure the space: it serves as the central point of the dwelling while separating the living room from a passageway that leads to the bedrooms. The design of this dwelling makes use of straight lines to determine the contrast between the materials and different transparent surfaces. The walls are white, as is the built-in furniture made from enameled wood and Corian. An exclusive selection of furniture completes the image by giving it a touch of color.

Cet appartement, situé au 14ᵉ étage d'un gratte-ciel de Milan, a été conçu sur l'idée d'un espace se propageant sans entrave. Les pièces sont disposées de telle sorte que les zones communes du logement communiquent avec les chambres privées sans qu'aucune séparation, ni murs ni portes fermées, n'interrompe cette continuité. Un module de cuisine indépendant sert à structurer l'espace : d'une part, il constitue en lui-même l'élément central du logement, et d'autre part, il sépare le salon d'un couloir qui conduit aux chambres. La conception de ce logement obéit à des lignes droites qui déterminent le contraste des matériaux et des différentes surfaces transparentes. Les murs sont blancs, une couleur que nous retrouvons sur les meubles encastrés en Corian et en bois laqué. Une sélection exclusive de mobilier vient compléter l'ensemble, y apportant une touche de couleur

Dieses Apartment im 14. Stockwerk eines Hochhauses in Mailand ist nach dem Konzept eines kontinuierlich fließenden Raumes gestaltet. Die Räume sind so angeordnet, dass der Weg vom öffentlicheren Bereich zu den privaten Räumen der Wohnung führt, ohne dass Grenzen, wie Wände und geschlossene Türen, diese Kontinuität unterbrechen. Ein frei in den Raum gestelltes Küchenelement dient der Strukturierung des Raumes: Einerseits bildet es selbst den Mittelpunkt der Wohnung, andererseits trennt es den Wohnbereich von einem Flur, der zu den Schlafräumen führt. Die Gestaltung der Wohnung ist von einer geraden Linienführung, dem Kontrast von Materialien und unterschiedlich transparenten Oberflächen bestimmt. Die Wände sind weiß, und auch die Einbaumöbel bestehen aus weiß lackiertem Holz und Corian. Eine exklusive Auswahl an Möbeln rundet das Bild ab und setzt farbliche Akzente.

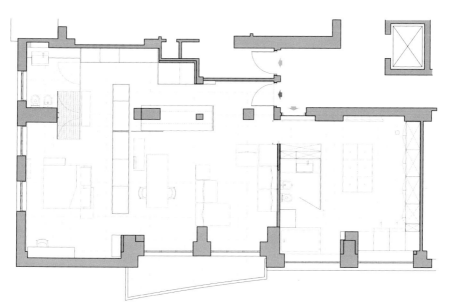

Plan Plan Grundriss

Two load-bearing columns, joined by the upper cabinet, are integrated in the kitchen island to form a sculptural unit.

Deux colonnes porteuses reliées par l'armoire supérieure sont intégrées au module de cuisine indépendant, formant une unité sculpturale.

In den freistehenden Küchenblock sind zwei tragende Stützen integriert. Der Oberschrank verbindet sie zu einer skulpturalen Einheit.

☐ Duplex in Dufaystraat

Dick van Gameren

This unusual duplex maisonette apartment was once an apparel store. Its triangular floor plan comes from the pointed shape of the building. When the owners bought the premises, the floor of the street-level store had already been removed, leaving only the back rooms, three feet higher, and the basement. During the conversion, it was decided that this split-level layout would be retained. The kitchen and dining room are on the lower level, next to a bedroom and bathroom. On the upper floor a study overlooks the street and there is a living room in the rear and a children's play room. A staircase near the entrance joins the two levels. The old shop window is now the main source of light. It was possible to maintain them complete in their original size because the upper floor is set back a good distance. In this way, the lower floor receives sufficient light.

Ce duplex insolite qui, à l'origine, était une ancienne boutique de vêtements, présente une base triangulaire du fait de la forme pointue du bâtiment. Lorsque les propriétaires achetèrent le local, le rez-de-chaussée, où se trouvait la boutique, avait été supprimé et il ne restait que les pièces arrière, situées un mètre au-dessus, et le sous-sol. On a décidé, au moment de la rénovation, de conserver cette distribution à différents niveaux. La cuisine et la salle à manger se trouvent désormais au niveau inférieur, ainsi qu'une chambre et une salle de bains. Le niveau supérieur comprend un bureau donnant sur la rue, un salon dans la partie arrière et une salle de jeu pour les enfants. Un escalier situé près de l'entrée relie les deux niveaux. L'ancienne vitrine fait office de source principale de lumière. Elle a pu être conservée entièrement, dans ses dimensions d'origine, étant donné que l'étage supérieur se situe en retrait par rapport à celle-ci. Ainsi, le niveau inférieur reçoit la lumière suffisante.

Diese ungewöhnliche Maisonette-Wohnung entstand aus einem ehemaligen Bekleidungsgeschäft, das durch die spitz zulaufende Form des Straßenblocks eine dreieckige Grundfläche aufweist. Als die Bauherren das Lokal kauften, war die Ladenebene auf Straßenniveau bereits entfernt, lediglich die etwa einen Meter höher gelegenen Hinterzimmer und die Kellerräume waren übriggeblieben. Beim Umbau wurde entschieden, diese Höhenverteilung beizubehalten. Im Untergeschoss befinden sich nun Küche und Essraum, daneben ein Schlafzimmer und ein Badezimmer. Im Obergeschoss liegt ein Arbeitszimmer zur Straße hin, ein Wohnraum zur Rückseite und ein Spielzimmer für die Kinder. Eine neben dem Eingang gelegene neue Treppe verbindet die beiden Ebenen miteinander. Das ehemalige Schaufenster dient als wichtigste Lichtquelle. Es konnte in voller Größe erhalten werden, weil das Obergeschoss in großem Abstand zu diesem gelegen ist. Auf diese Weise erhält das Unterschoss genügend Licht.

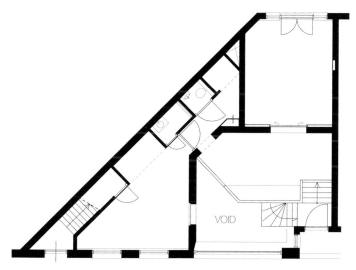

Upper level Niveau supérieur Obere Ebene

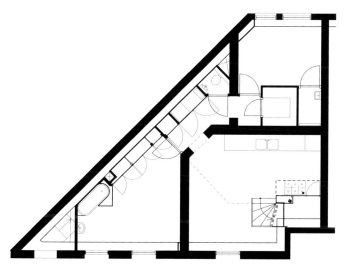

Lower level Niveau inférieur Untere Ebene

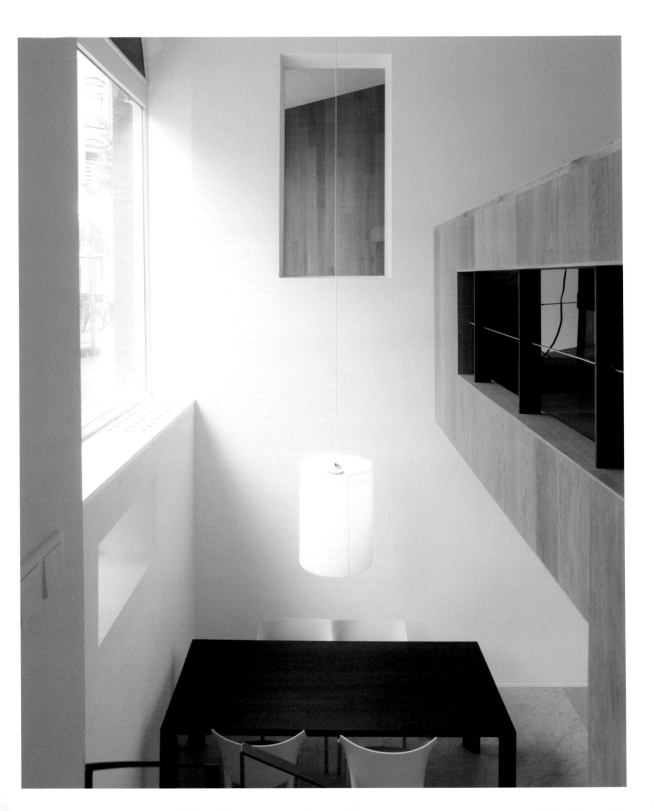

Plentiful light enters through the old shop window to the dining area, located on the lower level. This compensates for the disadvantage of having to be in the basement.

La lumière pénètre abondamment dans la salle à manger, située au niveau inférieur, à travers l'ancienne vitrine. On compense ainsi le fait qu'elle soit située au sous-sol.

Durch das ehemalige Schaufenster fällt reichlich Licht in den im Untergeschoss gelegenen Essbereich. Der Nachteil der Lage im Keller wird somit ausgeglichen.

☐ **Attic Apartment**

Geneviève Marginet

This small attic was designed as temporary accommodation while the house was refurbished. As it was only meant to be used for a short time, it was a good opportunity to try unusual and experimental design solutions. The futuristic sets of 60s and 70s movies served as inspiration, with their mix of straight lines and rounded corners, flat surfaces and horizontal emphasis. A three-dimensional form connects the living area, kitchen and bathroom. The range, microwave oven and kitchen and bathroom cabinets have been placed in different openings and cavities that remind one of the doors of travel trailers, airplanes and space ships, and accentuate the transitory nature of this small apartment. A steep folding ladder gives access to the upper level where there is a sleeping loft and a desk with a shape similar to the counter that serves as a dining table on the lower level.

Cet appartement sur les toits a été conçu comme une habitation provisoire, afin de pouvoir se loger pendant la rénovation de la maison. Étant donné que sa durée d'utilisation allait être assez courte, cela laissait toute liberté pour avoir recours à des solutions expérimentales et insolites. La scénographie futuriste des films des années 60 et 70 servit d'inspiration, avec son mélange caractéristique de lignes droites et d'angles arrondis, ses surfaces planes et son horizontalité. Un élément tridimensionnel relie le salon, la cuisine et la salle de bains. La cuisinière, le four, le micro-ondes et les meubles de la cuisine et de la salle de bains ont été placés dans différents orifices et cavités, qui rappellent les portes des caravanes, des avions et des navettes spatiales, ce qui accentue le côté provisoire de cette petite habitation. Une échelle pliante assez raide permet d'accéder au niveau supérieur, où se trouvent la chambre et un bureau, dont la forme ressemble au comptoir qui sert de table de salle à manger au niveau inférieur.

Diese kleine Dachwohnung wurde als temporäre Wohnung entworfen, die als Unterkunft dienen sollte, als das Haus saniert wurde. Da sie nur kurze Zeit bewohnt werden sollte, gab es eine große Bereitschaft zu ungewöhnlichen, experimentellen Lösungen. Als Inspiration dienten die futuristischen Filmarchitekturen der 1960er und 1970er Jahre mit ihrer charakteristischen Mischung aus geraden Linien und runden Ecken, ihrer Flächigkeit und Horizontalität. Eine dreidimensionale Form verbindet Wohnraum, Küche und Badezimmer. In unterschiedlichen Öffnungen und Hohlräumen, die an Türen von Campingfahrzeugen, Flugzeugen und Raumschiffen erinnern und so den transitorischen Charakter der kleinen Wohnung betonen, werden Herd und Ofen, Mikrowelle, Küchen- und Badezimmerschränke platziert. Über eine steile Faltleiter erreicht man die oben gelegene Schlafebene mit einem Arbeitstisch, der in seiner Form der des Küchentresens im Untergeschoss ähnelt.

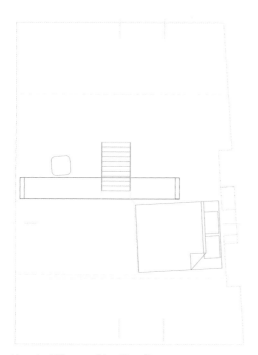

Upper level Niveau supérieur Obere Ebene

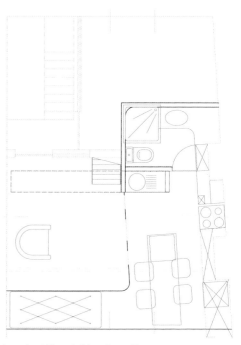

Lower level Niveau inférieur Untere Ebene

Photo credits

p. 10-19   CJ Studio

p. 20-27   Filippo Bombace

p. 28-37   MoHen Design International

p. 38-47   Michael Boland

p. 48-55   Carlos Cezanne

p. 56-67   Philip Tang

p. 68-73   Popeye Tsang

p. 74-83   Fernandes Capanema Arquitetura

p. 84-91   Pedro M. Mamahud

p. 92-99   John M. Hall

p. 100-107   Ryota Aratashi

p. 108-115   Peter Ebner

p. 116-125   Pablo Fernández Lorenzo

p. 126-135   Carlos Domínguez

p. 136-143   Javier Haddad Conde

p. 144-153   Gogortza & Llorella

p. 154-161   Philippe Harden

p. 162-169   Andrea Martiradonna

p. 170-179   Luuk Kramer

p. 180-189   Vercruysse & Dujardin/Owi Bz

P. 191   Gogortza & Llorella